DRAGONHEARTS

POEMS & PROSE BY

NIKITA GILL
AMANDA LOVELACE
TRISTA MATEER

dragonhearts

ISBN-13: 978-1-793-14945-9

Editor: Mira Kennedy
Designer: Amanda Lovelace & Trista Mateer
Interior Art: Trista Mateer
Cover Font: Trista Mateer
Cover Photo: Lauren Zaknoun
laurenzaknoun.com

to anyone who is looking for a home for their heart:
may you let it rest on these pages.

trigger warning:

intimate partner violence, intimate partner abuse,
child abuse, emotional abuse, stalking, queerphobia,
sexism, mental health issues, body image issues,
bullying, trauma, death, violence,
fire, blood, & gore.

remember to practice self-care
before, during, & after reading.

what does being a dragonheart mean to you?

surviving / having flames in your veins / never-ending loyalty / powerful alone & with like-hearted people / loving fiercely / strong-spined / dangerous / celebrating yourself / celebrating others / magic even without spells / protective / gentle but armored / light-giver / reigning supremely / what fairy tales are made of / queen of your own life / no doubts about your own worth / forever valiant / tower-breaker / kingdom-shaker / standing up for others / resisting over & over / taking charge of your narrative / bravery beyond measure / not giving negativity a seat at your table / facing the fire head-on / prioritizing yourself / story-hungry / made of gold / dream-chaser / sea storm courage / voice-reclaimer / war-hearted / flower-hearted / RELENTLESS

You are never ever truly breaking. There is nothing about you that must fit into a mold, yet the world keeps trying to mold you, shove you into a box, act like this is all that you are. Imagine how ridiculous they must seem to anyone looking in from across the universe. Trying to shove a whole galaxy into a box and stamp the word *normal* onto it, as if it was just going to stay put, as if it won't just burst through any container it is put into. You are simply doing what all galaxies are inclined to do. You are shattering the thing that holds you in. Remember that.

by Nikita Gill

sinking further into myself / becoming small / Russian doll creature / onion climbing back inside her layers / he put his hands on me and I turned docile / lost touch with my friends / locked up my shoes and coat / he plied me with tea and honey / and I grew too lazy to lift a hand in defense of myself / I didn't forget my own name but I forgot other things / watched the sun come up / chugged NyQuil before crawling into bed next to him / called it a sleeping potion / over the counter magic / his breath in the bed made me nervous until it didn't / I never really shook the nerves / just the urgency / got complacent and called it love / let my body wither under my own care / I put curlers in while he was at work / I made small talk with his mother / watched the way she moved through the house / and ghosted after her / specter in a nightgown washing dishes / baking pies / contemplating death at the kitchen table / I thought domesticity was an illness until I realized I was sick on bad love / by the time I left I was clawing out of my own skin / aching for a moment of beauty that had nothing to do with my body

by Trista Mateer

2

Become fluent in the language of letting go. Learn to give people up before they hurt you beyond repair. Even if they tell you that they will change. Even if they tell you that they love you. Just remember, love isn't meant to be permanently damaging. Love is meant to aid your healing.

by Nikita Gill

ON BEING STALKED

Roses smashed on the front porch. Bobby pins mailed back one by one. A shadow is just a shadow until it starts to scare you. A man is just a man until he reaches for your throat. Until he watches you from parked cars and street corners. Slits your tires. Shows up at your job. Follows you out of town. So yes,

                    YES.

        I set aside my quiet.
        I bought a pocket knife.
        I shrieked at him on the street.
        I caused a scene at every
        public place he showed up.

People called it unladylike, said he was just acting out of love, said men were animals but I was *crazy*. Maybe they were right, but I felt powerless until the day I realized that hell is a place other people put you and I could put us

                both

                                there.

by Trista Mateer

Hellfire

You
sad
achey
thing,
mouth twisted
like the wretch
he made you.

Take out
your capped
tooth
and spread
the cyanide
over any earth
he touched,

bite each bruise
until it's yours
and yours alone.

Spit love back
at them
like it's full of acid,
like hell is a place
that you are always
walking back out of,
not a scratch on you.

by Caitlyn Siehl

so many scaled my tower, / swore to slay the beast in exchange for me— / their prize. / despite their confidence, / they simply lacked the strength to take the beast down. / in the end, / i was the one who climbed the pile of the fallen, / took hold of a bloodied sword, / slashed open both our chests, / & placed its heart right beside mine— / my prize.

- *dragonhearted.*
by amanda lovelace

WHEN THEY EXPECT

beauty,

GIVE THEM

BEAST.

— DRAGONHEART RULE #1

ANYWAY HERE'S WONDERWALL
blackout poem adapted from "Wonderwall" by Oasis

I don't believe

you're gonna
save   me

I   m

gonna

save
me

by Trista Mateer

9

In this story, the princess runs away from her tower and into the woods. She runs and she runs until she can't anymore. She left the walls that caused her such pain but those walls offered protection as well and out here in the world, everything is sharp. She gets sharp, too, after a while. Barbed tongue and bristles. She draws blood when she has to and sometimes when she doesn't.

In this story, nothing ends at the drawbridge.

In this story, there is character development.

In this story, escaping your tormentor isn't enough to save you; it's just enough to keep you alive.

by Trista Mateer

you are a primordial thing. nyx herself created you from her mother chaos, sent you down to earth to show the world how courage lives even in places you least expect it. you are a fire crafted from goddess hands. you know how to smile & dare demons & gods alike. so when they tell you that you are weak or small or something insignificant, know this: you could win even mythological battles with your ferocity.

- *you predate athena.*
by Nikita Gill and amanda lovelace

Time's Up

Who says that princesses cannot be wolves and that women must be light without a shadow? Maybe a witch is just a woman who knows how to harness her powerful voice. Who says you must be silent so that you can thrive? Silence is not the price you have to pay for your survival anymore.

Speak.
Scream.
Roar.

by Nikita Gill

you will never allow a tower or a dungeon to contain you.

— DRAGONHEART RULE #2

13

if it feels better to run into the wildwood, then do it. just don't forget to bring your crown with you. let your hair get tangled up in it. rule the treetops above you & the dirt beneath your feet, if you must. build your own castle from the ash & bone of all those who told you there were limits to what your hands could do.

- you're much too victorious to give up.
by amanda lovelace & Trista Mateer

armies see you
dancing down
that warpath
from miles away
& decide to surrender
because they know
they wouldn't
stand a fucking chance
against you.

- *no sword necessary.*
by amanda lovelace

be both
regal & terrifying.

keep them forever
on their toes.

- don't let them force you into a box.
by amanda lovelace

Your scars are a warning to all future monsters of the hell you have survived before them, every demon you have vanquished, and every battle you have won.

by Nikita Gill

i
used to
call myself
a

           lioness.

now
the lioness
bows her head,
tells me she
wishes she had
a bite like
mine.

- *strength.*
by amanda lovelace

SHE OF THE WOODS

Swamp creature. All unwashed mouth, all river mud. You overgrown bramble. You outrageous thorn. Unafraid of a little blood. Unafraid of a lot. Opposition trembles before you. Runs away and tells stories of your unholiness. Your dirt and your anger. All your bite. Reputation doesn't precede you; it follows you around with its tail between its legs. It cowers in your shadow. Curse the words of those who tried to bury you. Bless your inability to stay down.

by Trista Mateer

I'm in love with my anger / my
war-won body / tense and vicious.

by Trista Mateer

you are not dripping in things such as gold or jewels or riches. no—you are dripping with the red, red blood of every misguided prince/princess/royal who made you think that they were the only means to your freedom. little do they know, you will rule over the very tower that once oppressed you.

- keep turning tables.
by amanda lovelace

Queens

"What is a queen without her king?"

I don't know,
but let's ask
Cleopatra,
Nefertiti,
Hatshepsut,
Sammuramat,
Victoria,
Elizabeth,
Amina,
Tzu-hsi,
and the countless other kingless queens
who turned mere kingdoms
into the greatest of empires.

by Nikita Gill

Queens II

Listen to me, girl:
you have castles inside your bones,
coronets in your heart.
If he threatens you with battle,
you raise him a whole war.
The last time I checked,
queens cower before no man.

by Nikita Gill

THINGS THAT AREN'T REQUIRED
TO BE A QUEEN:

a crown
a castle
a king
mercy
womanhood

by amanda lovelace & Trista Mateer

Rebel soft. Steel and Saponaria. Honey-tongued and unapologetic. I will not give up the flowers in my heart for stones just because the world is a hard place. The world is only hard because it needs more flower-hearted people.

by Nikita Gill

who said you can't
wear a flower crown
& still remain a
fearsome thing?

- *make persephone proud.*
by amanda lovelace

Forget what you know about strength. Sensitivity is powerful. And sometimes silence isn't. Sometimes rebellion looks a lot like crying. Sometimes it looks like the softest thing you've ever seen. Sometimes survival is the act of getting out of bed. The idea that strength is exactly the same for every person is an untrue one. People are strong in different ways. The expression of emotion doesn't mean you are weak; it means you wear your strength differently. We all do.

by Nikita Gill

POEM IN WHICH NOBODY IS A MOON

I thought for a long time that if I wasn't orbiting around Venus, I'd just be drifting aimlessly through my life without a purpose. Never stopped to wonder why I felt like I needed a purpose. Never stopped to wonder why I thought romantic love was the greatest thing I could do with my life. Never stopped to wonder why my life needed to be great and couldn't just be

lived.

by Trista Mateer

throw entire festivals in your name. invite no one but yourself. let there be choirs, let there be lanterns, let there be games, let there be cake, let there be laughter, let there be fireworks. some people make the mistake of spending their lives waiting for other people to celebrate their victories, so they never end up celebrating them at all. don't wait for anyone to decide that you're enough. you've endured every minute up until now—isn't that just remarkable?

- isn't it?
by amanda lovelace

What do you do
when your world falls apart
and you must confront
the most wounded
part of yourself?

You hurt.
You ache.
You throb.
You cleanse.
You purify.
You heal.

by Nikita Gill

Honest Facts I Have Learned About People

1. We are all 65-70% water.
2. We are all stardust.
3. We all suffer,
   but we do not have to suffer alone.

by Nikita Gill

DON'T BE AFRAID
TO STRAY FROM

the path

OF ANYTHING THAT
ISN'T MEANT FOR YOU

— DRAGONHEART RULE #3

in this story, the princess gives up her title & trades it in for *warrior*; by her definition, someone who fights for the good of themselves & only themselves. so badly she wants it to fit, but no matter how much she wiggles around inside of it, it still feels like a corset laced too tightly. when she can scarcely breathe, two like-hearted souls come along, ask her why they can't all be equal parts *warrior* & *princess*. why can't they defend themselves & those who need it the most?

she doesn't have a good answer for them.

- *she has only trust for them in her heart.*
by amanda lovelace

The Light
after Iain S. Thomas

Humans are bad at most things. Love, relationships, parenting, holding ourselves together, being dependable. But there is one thing we are so good at, that we are, in fact, spectacular at it. We are all so damned good at being broken open. It's how the light gets out. It's how we know it's there. Because once in a while, someone comes along who tells us life is so much more than just existing. Someone comes along to remind us to stop being so small and so human. And do better by being so much more.

by Nikita Gill

I stand over the sink in your first apartment, the knife in my hand making firm and deliberate strokes when I press it against the fruit in my palm. It's safer to do this on a cutting board but I don't know where you store them and I don't want to ask. I make it all the way through your mango and halfway through mine before I slice my hand right across my lifeline. The knife does not clatter onto the counter. The fruit does not slip from my grasp. I breathe through it. Turn the sink on. Run my hand under the cold water. Shove a piece of mango in my mouth and wince around the juice. I'm not ready for you to see me bleed. I'm not ready for you to know I am a fallible thing.

by Trista Mateer

you need not bleed for me. you need not leave fruit at my altar. i accept no blood oaths, no special offerings. my loyalty to you is not something you can spell out of thin air with a rose quartz & a pink candle. when it's there, it's there—no exceptions. it will never allow itself to fade, either.

- *the most powerful witch couldn't banish it.*
by amanda lovelace

I used to only pick up a pen for myself
but now
I pick one up for you too.

Is there such a thing
as an unselfish love poem?
I don't know,

but I'm trying.

by Trista Mateer

in a hushed voice you tell me,
> *"fairy tales still make me cry."*

i tell you,
> *"that isn't a weak spot."*

i tell you,
> *"it's part of what makes you magick."*

- *salt water.*
by amanda lovelace

LOST GIRL

Little thing running through the woods chasing elves and hobgoblins, smearing berries across my face and sharpening the points of hawthorn branches into makeshift swords. I carried salt in my pockets. I pried nails out of the floorboards. I built a world where no one could keep up with me. I made a myth out of myself in my youth and spent the rest of my life trying to claw my way back.

by Trista Mateer

The first lioness I followed around wasn't my mother. It was Alanna, lady knight with her sword and her steed. I carried those books everywhere. I traced my hands over Tamora Pierce's name on the cover and dreamt of princesses and spywork. I dreamt of ships and deserts. I dreamt of warriors and then I grew into one. I quested over oceans. I drew blood and I will draw it again.

All my childhood heroes lived on the page.

Now they live in me.

by Trista Mateer

Why We March, We Cry, We Protest

To all the little girls out there:
we will set fire to this world
that steals your childhoods,
rips away your choices and voices,
and stops you from being
everything you want to be,
and build you a better one
from the embers,
the kind of world that treasures you
for all your powerful capabilities.

by Nikita Gill

Sometimes it feels like there is no magic in a world where the bad guys always seem to win. But there is. In every act of kindness and bravery, there is the magic we all seek.

by Nikita Gill

FIND YOUR PEOPLE &
IF YOU CAN'T BUILD CASTLES
WITH THEM, THEN BUILD HOMES.

— DRAGONHEART RULE #4

I dug into hillsides.
I knocked on trees.
I pressed my palms to the back
of every wardrobe.

I tried for years
to find my way into magical worlds.

Now I just try to weave magic
into this one.

by Trista Mateer

Upstairs, the gentle sobbing of my mother, the heaving of her chest because I'm not beautiful like she wanted me to be. I take her hand, palm-up, and make her feel the hair on my face until she yanks herself away.

She called it disgusting once but now she just says nothing. She buys me shapewear and Dolce & Gabbana perfume and three different kinds of depilatory creams that smell like chemicals and leave my face red but not smooth. I keep taking her hand, palm-up, to remind her that it's there. I shave it and it grows back—like me, so stubborn under all that makeup.

I lure myself into a spandex trap and I text Amanda, "Is this what death feels like?" Alone in my room I say, "God, is this a poem? It's uncomfortable. It feels like a poem." God never answers, which is what really makes it poetry.

I pull on Spanx and think of death and when I'm done thinking of death, I think of God, and when I'm done thinking of God, I fall backwards onto my bed and try to feel small. It isn't hard.

I think of my mother upstairs.

And then God doesn't answer, but Amanda does.

by Trista Mateer

my spiraling thoughts are keeping me up late. again. i text her & i'm surprised to find that she's still awake. she texts back to let me know that she's being haunted too, & how she guesses that means we're haunted together. for the first time in months, i sleep without needing some source of light.

- *i am never alone when i have you.*
by amanda lovelace

She never tells me that my ghosts aren't real.

by Trista Mateer

you are my favorite spellbook.

- all of your pages are bewitching.
by amanda lovelace & Trista Mateer

"just say the word," she tells me.

there is something awe-inspiring
about the way she always rushes in,
arrows blazing, ready to
defend my honor.

she knows i've got this.

i have dozens of scars
to prove my resilience
& i trusted her enough
to show them to her.

"just say it," she tells me.

she only wants
to reassure me she
would throw herself
to the wolves regardless.

- *huntress.*
by amanda lovelace

we call ourselves solitary witches. as in *no, we don't need anyone else to define our magick.* as in *neither of us have ever trusted anyone enough to give them that.* then we go into the other room & shut the door. we hold hands. we spill salt. we hum hymns. it's all so easy. we're powerful all on our own; as one, something to warn others about.

- i forget that we didn't know each other, once.
by amanda lovelace

The Coven

When they break your heart,
run to a sister who will stroke your hair
and remind you of what you are.

When no one else understands,
run to a sister who will hold you close
and heal you with the kindest words.

When the wound is fresh,
your sisters are the only ones
who know how to enchant away the pain.

When a man scares you enough to choke
on your own tears, text your sisters
and they will hex him into hell for you.

This is what covens will do:
protect each other from the world,
for this is what sisters do.

by Nikita Gill

I say, *I felt unstoppable in love.*
What if I never get back there?

You say, *you'll get somewhere else.*
There are so many other things to be.

by Trista Mateer

SPELL FOR SELF-LOVE

ingredients:
- 1 pink candle
- 1 match
- 1 rose quartz point
- water
- red rose petals
- ¼ cup pink himalayan salt
- 3-5 drops orange essential oil

directions:
1. fill bathtub with warm water.
2. mix orange essential oil with pink himalayan salt. throw into bathwater. add red rose petals as desired. stir all contents clockwise.
3. light pink candle with match.
4. place rose quartz next to candle.
5. as you soak, stare into the flame & feel yourself begin to relax. take deep, calming breaths & imagine your lungs are being filled with love, light, & power.
6. picture your worries melting away with the salt & being replaced by both self-confidence & self-assurance.
7. remember that you don't need this ritual to experience self-love; the magick is already inside you.

by amanda lovelace & Trista Mateer

56

GET YOUR HANDS

DIRTY.

unearth

YOUR MAGIC.

— DRAGONHEART RULE #5

she is the one i crawl to whenever i feel like i'm on the verge of collapsing. she says to me, "they don't know that you are the sea & the sea takes shit from no one." what i wish i said back is, "if that's true & i am the sea, then it's only because you make me feel powerful enough to take on most of the world."

- *you make me so much better.*
by amanda lovelace

Diwali

In India, we have a festival of lights,
a celebration that illuminates whole cities
and towns; everything burns & burns bright.
And this one day, we are not afraid of fire.
The fire is the auspicious thing. We say:
"The Goddess is coming home to us;
she brings wealth to our houses and hearts."
This is how I see my sisters. Pure as fire,
the greatest wealth I could ever know,
finally, finally, bringing me home.

by Nikita Gill

THINGS I LEARNED FROM NIKITA GILL:

1. My heart is as vast and deep as the fucking ocean and I deserve better than lovers who fear drowning.
2. There is a spell for almost anything and if there's not a spell, there is at least a poem.
3. When she lets her hair loose and wears her anger like a crown, her rage rivals that of gods. So does her tenderness. Both are allowed to coexist in the same body loudly and without shame.
4. My hands are so small that it takes two of mine to hold one of hers. So we're not a perfect fit. So we weren't made for each other and we found each other anyway. Isn't that stranger? Isn't that better?

by Trista Mateer

I named the bluebells in my garden after you and they all sprouted up stronger because of it. Look how my love for you makes things grow.

by Trista Mateer

The gods are fickle. The universe is completely random in the way it functions. But you know what we can do to make sense of the randomness? Be kind to each other. Help each other. Bring each other peace. I spoke to Persephone last night, and even the dreaded queen of the Underworld agrees.

by Nikita Gill

In another life, I might have named a sword after you, an axe or a bow. I might have drawn blood for you and enjoyed it. / But in this life, I watch you laugh in the beachgrass. We pluck bayberries from the dunes. I sing your name over the sand and we dance, giddy, across the waves with no knowledge of what might have come before or what might come after.

by Trista Mateer

TEMPORARY HOME

On the page there is always a place for us. No oceans to stand in the way. No distance to cross. This isn't why we write but it's part of it. A place for our ivyhands to finally stop reaching. Here, we wind our words together until no one can tell our stories apart.

by Trista Mateer

I have turned this life into a kinder thing than what I was given. With these hands, I fashioned the ashes of its cruelty into clay and turned that clay into the bones of the thing I wanted it to be. Come and see how I have tamed the monster that once tried to kill the good in me.

by Nikita Gill

In this story,
the battles that are fought alone
aren't always lost,

but they're lost more often
than the battles that are fought
together.

by Trista Mateer

DON'T LET THE OLD TALES FOOL YOU

Monsters aren't always easy to spot. Yellow eyes and claws at the ready. Gruesome mouths and matted fur. No. They can wear the faces of our friends. They can share our blood. The truth is, everyone has either loved a monster or been one, and sometimes both. There is nothing more dangerous than the thing that lives inside of you, waiting for love to wrong you, waiting to make prey out of someone else.

We all have it in us to be monstrous and there is still no excuse for monstrosity.

If we want to be the heroes of our own stories, and more than heroic—if we want to be *good*—we must face down the thing that lives inside of us. Commit to unpacking our anger in empty rooms. Understand our treacherous impulses and act against them, continuously.

by Nikita Gill and Trista Mateer

there will always be people who refuse to treat you the way you deserve. there will be jealousy. there will be malice. there will be pettiness. oh, plenty of it to go around. as you smile, unbothered, let them know how much better off you are without their venom coursing through your veins.

- *treat your wounds.*
by amanda lovelace

throw
their names
into the
blazing
cauldron.

wish away
anyone
who
makes you
feel

anything less
than the
eighth wonder
of the
world.

- *banishment.*
by amanda lovelace

BANISH
self-hatred
MANIFEST
self-love

— DRAGONHEART RULE #6

Cutting toxic people out of your life may be hard, but it's incredibly freeing. Even the air tastes sweeter because you're no longer breathing through their poisonous fumes. Ask Hades when he let go of his brothers. Even in the Underworld, the air suddenly honeyed, made his reign feel so much kinder, better than it ever was before.

by Nikita Gill

if they cannot handle your ugliest truths, then you don't need them in your life. the ones who truly love & support you will never try to silence you or invalidate your suffering. breathe in the disappointment; breathe it back out in the form of

"goodbye, my love."

- *some paths are alone but not lonely.*
by amanda lovelace

When they tuck your hair behind your ear
and call you *wild*,

what they mean is:
you are something to be tamed.
Something to show off at parties.
Sharp tongue on a leash.
Claws clipped neatly.
Feral creature whittled down to
almost nothing.
It makes them feel a little free,
to kiss something dangerous on the mouth.
It satisfies them to hobble something
powerful.

Don't let it hold you down.
Remember how viciously you lived
when you were untouched.

by Trista Mateer

i let her call me *wild one*. she's seen all the same trees i've seen. she knows what it is to be hunted the way i've been hunted.

- doe.
by amanda lovelace

save energy by picking & choosing your battles with great care. before you decide it's time to put on your armor & draw your blade, remember your limitations. by respecting them, you, in turn, respect yourself.

- fully charged.
by amanda lovelace & Trista Mateer

go to the closet. take hold of your broomstick. open your backdoor as wide as it can go. sweep out every particle of dust & negative energy that dares to enter your space uninvited. remember the old saying: *negativity begets negativity, while positivity begets positivity.* don't you dare let the universe hear you put yourself down again. more going easy on yourself; more believing that impossibly wonderful things can & will happen to you.

- enjoy this messy, messy journey.
by amanda lovelace

Try Me

And the sun glared at the girl
who burned as bright as him,
and asked, "Who told you that
you could compete with me?"

She grinned, "Not a soul.
They all simply told me that
I couldn't gleam like you
and I just said, so dare me."

by Nikita Gill

do it.

eat the
forbidden fruit,
punishment be
damned.

do it on purpose.

because
they think you don't
have it in you
to wreak havoc.

do it even if you're not hungry.

make them regret
telling you
what you can
& cannot have.

- *pomegranate.*
by amanda lovelace

YOUR SELF-CARE MIGHT BE *roses* MIGHT BE

AND THEIRS MIGHT BE *thorns*

— DRAGONHEART RULE #7

Honeylight

The day I stopped naming this body *cage*
and a thing that no one could ever love,
the darkness learned to fear me
and flee so I could finally dip my body
in the honeylight glow of my own soft,
warm, gentle love.

by Nikita Gill

What I Weigh
inspired by the I Weigh movement

I weigh the sea.
I weigh the storm.
I weigh a thousand stories long.
I weigh my mother's fortitude and my father's eyes.
I weigh how they look at me with pride.
I weigh strength and fearlessness and the warrior in me.
I weigh all the pain and trauma that made me see
that I have more galaxies inside me than tragedies.
We all weigh joys and darkness and goodness and sin.
You see, we are infinite within this skin we are in.
So when they ask you what you weigh,
you don't need to look down at any scale.
Instead, simply tell them the truth;
tell them how you
weigh whole universes
and storms and scars and stories, too.

by Nikita Gill

demand the heart
of anyone
who dares to
laugh in your face
& call you
a *silly, pretty thing*
when you say
you feel like
you could rule
everything
if someone only
gave you the
chance.

- you are already the queen of it all.
by amanda lovelace

know when
you need to
draw your lines
in the sand.

know when
you need to
lock your windows
& your doors.

know when
you need to
put your
fences up.

(& when
you need to
lace them with
barbed wire.)

truth is,
we have control
over very little
in this life,

but we
have every say
in who gets
our love.

- *boundarie*s.
by amanda lovelace

Your existence has never been the apology they want you to think it is. Don't let anyone impede your journey by forcing you to suppress your pain just so they can be more comfortable.

by Nikita Gill

If there is a tower inside me,
then she didn't show up on a white horse
and scale the walls.

She counted the bricks.
She took my hand
and showed me her own stones.

by Trista Mateer

You are the only people who ever really see me.
We are always in the act of coming home to each other.

by Trista Mateer

In this house, we write response poems
to our friends' poems. We never have

to look too far for a pen. There are always
notebooks in boxes and desk drawers, but

we still run to the corner shop to buy new
ones anyway. In this house, everything is

hyperbole and metaphor. Someone is
always crying, but someone is always

singing, too. There's so much noise and
none of it keeps me up at night.

by Trista Mateer

millions of life cycles from now,
i think i'll be a whale.

maybe you'll be a whale, too,
or maybe you'll be a seal.

i just know that
no matter where you are,

i will sing for you until
you swim back to me.

i will sing for you until
you come back home.

- *i promise this to you.*
by amanda lovelace

THREE OF SWORDS (REVERSED)

Both of us are
putting our best foot forward,
learning how to forgive
and practicing on each other.

I know what love looks like now
because I've seen it on your face.

by Trista Mateer

I am growing up.
I am getting better.
I am healing
even when I'm not writing poems about it.
Some things are just done off the page.

by Trista Mateer

My survival is still the loudest and most honest thing I have ever done to show myself how much I love myself.

by Nikita Gill

STAR EMOJI
a poem crafted out of texts I've sent to my friends
after "Heart Emoji" by Lyd Havens

HI I LOVE YOU / I just didn't see you yesterday so my
heart is screaming / but it's always / screaming about
something / I woke up from a dream about you / I just
woke up from a dream about running through a grocery
store with you, trying to find duck sauce / I had a dream
that I was on a train and you were running to the station
with your shoes in your hands / your graduation photos
make it look like you attended Hogwarts / you're a big
part of the magic / in my life / I'm so proud of you / I
am literally always wishing the best for you / you could
read a grocery list and I'd call it a poem / queen of my
heart / yes / star of my heart / yes / light of my life / yes
/ you own a fucking sword, I don't expect you to be this
tender / I'm going to have to stop calling it lowkey /
everything I feel is so loud / I have more to say than
poetry allows sometimes / but I'm so happy you're
happy / there are words / at least / for that

by Trista Mateer

romantic love

DOESN'T HAVE TO BE
THE MAIN PLOT OF

your story.

— DRAGONHEART RULE # 8

Monterey, CA

We drove across the country
and you took pictures of the
flowers in fairy gardens,
you let me make your coffee too
sweet, you waited outside of every
gas station while I bought
banana nut muffins

and I wasn't some
untouched, unlovable thing.

I was brave and
you were with me
and I stopped screaming
long enough to realize
that love was nothing
compared to helping you
name your poems in the car,
eating Dippin' Dots
with you on the pier,
buying Hot Pockets
and German chocolate brownies
and spreading them out across
motel beds,

missing nothing
because we had everything.

by Caitlyn Siehl

JOY RIDE

sunday morning, the hushed walk out of the dorm /
your tiny beetle car hanging on / by our giggling
prayers / filling up the gas, half ready to explode / the
drive two towns over / parking in a church parking lot
because god would never / no seats in the coffee shop /
no ginger ale in the pizzeria / william faulkner's words
to read but / you're falling in love & / i'm full of
blessings / we turn off our phones because we hate /
everyone & yell it so with the windows down / our icy
fingertips because we didn't think ahead / because joy
is best unplanned / we get sick right after this / as if no
fraction of girlhood can go without punishment / but
even then, feverish & delirious, you / are the voice on
the other side of the wall / the body in the car / the
person bearing witness to my heart & rage / you could
tell this story in my voice / & maybe even i wouldn't
hear the difference, except / you wouldn't / except you
love my voice.

by Yena Sharma Purmasir

when we were little girls, we rode broomsticks around the backyard, wishing we were playing something much more magical than basketball or dodgeball. we threw gems into the deep end of the pool, wishing we were mermaids on the hunt for their stolen treasure. we fell asleep holding hands, wishing our souls would roam faraway lands together. never—not even once— did you tell me there was something in this world i couldn't do.

- *i will never forget you.*
by amanda lovelace

PRIDE

Nobody ever told me that I could build my own family. Take out the parts that didn't accept me and replace them with kinder models. Replace them with people who went out in June to buy multi-colored cups and glitter. People who argued over how to make rainbow cake but still made the cake. Still got the icing on and sprinkles too. Laughed over the mess of it all. Wide-mouthed and grinning. Momentarily forgetting the part of the world that would rather we kept to our cramped, quiet cupboards underneath the stairs.

by amanda lovelace & Trista Mateer

NO SECRETS

There are chambers in me full of flowers and there are chambers in me full of fire. Or maybe heartburn. Or maybe anger. It's hard to tell most days. There are so many doors in my chest and I've given you keys to all of them.

by Trista Mateer

When you wake night after night to the sounds of tree limbs tapping on your window and your wishful heart mistakes them for hands, there is no shame in it. The wanting to escape. The restless sleep. Your storybook-soul laying open on the bedroom floor. This world is not for everyone but there are worlds for everyone. Sometimes you just have to chase a star or two to find them.

by Trista Mateer

we bonded over our love for good stories. / we wanted nothing more than to grow up to be just like the girls with swords, / the girls with arrows, / the girls with sharp teeth, / the girls with wands, / the girls who dreamed of saving the day, / & the girls who never wanted to be heroes. / now that we're all grown up, / it has to be said: / no writer could conjure up a character with the strength to match ours.

- *for the story-hungry ones.*
by amanda lovelace

Palat (पलट)

You see a beautiful girl who makes you feel like
a beautiful girl, sits next to you on the charter bus
and tells you her life story. Some loves are so small
they only last eight weeks. Some are so heavy
they cover childhood trauma in one night, hiding
in the library while everyone else is sleeping under
the stars. You don't consider the weight until
you're trying to pack your suitcase home and find
that you can't possibly fold down two months of joy.
You get so used to hearing someone's laughter across
tent hill, you start believing halfway across America
is no different. The last time you saw her,
she was walking towards airport security.
Do you remember how in those old Bollywood movies,
the ones that bonded you to a one-time stranger,
they said that if someone really loved you,
they would turn around just one last time?
Do you remember how you felt when she waved?

by Yena Sharma Purmasir

Certain people genuinely believe they are halves out looking for what will make them whole. But people aren't halves. We are all small universes out finding other universes to collide into. We are always two wholes coming together by choice. Never halves.

by Nikita Gill

GRATITUDE

for seeing me through my first UTI / for holding my hand while I broke my own heart / for giving up your bed / for sharing your books / for building a home with me / for feeding my cat / for making dinner / for the adventures / the sugar in its bowl / the poems you read over the phone / for all the motel beds we slept in / the continental breakfasts / the space when I needed it / for learning the words to my favorite songs / for always driving / for never making me feel ashamed / for reading my poems before anyone else / here's to our soft domestic lives and the fire-eaters who live them / thanks for the light in my eyes / you put it there

by Trista Mateer

Thank you for showing me what home looks like. With your talent, with your kindness, with your wisdom, with your warrior strength. Thank you for giving this nowhere girl a piece of your heart, a somewhere to let her guard down and understand what it truly means to find a soulhome.

by Nikita Gill

A Witch's Fairytale
for amanda lovelace and Trista Mateer

Bring me your wounds.
Bring me the pain.
Bring me any ache
you cannot spell away.
Bring me the tragedies you never forget about.
Bring me heartache and doubt.

It is good to be your sister during times
when the weather is sunny and sweet.
But it is a privilege to be your sister
when you share your storms with me.

by Nikita Gill

the thing about storms
is that they have the power
to help things grow
or drown them.

we're the same.

bring the lightning
& i'll bring the thunder;
together, we will create
such gentle wreckage.

- *the storm-callers.*
by amanda lovelace & Trista Mateer

when we are together.

when we are holding onto
each other, laughing.

when we forget all the pain
that brought us together
in the first place.

- *what love stories are made of.*
by amanda lovelace

WRITE THE
FAIRYTALE ENDING

that you deserve.

— DRAGONHEART RULE #9

when they were afraid of what we could do if we ran wild, of what we could do without asking their permission first, they set fire to our magick while our loved ones watched from a cheering crowd. now, what's done is done, dear one. you just need to make sure the world never has the chance to forget the terror we stir when we have the bravery to stand up for ourselves. even more so when we dare to stand together, hand in hand.

- *be nothing if not relentless.*
by amanda lovelace

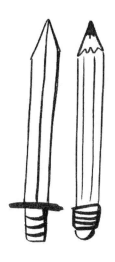

a note from the authors

dragonhearts started as the brain-child of
amanda lovelace. the concept was originally used in the
bonus chapter of the barnes & noble exclusive
hardcover of *the witch doesn't burn in this one*.
none of the poems from that chapter appear in
this book but they did inspire its creation.

some of these poems may have previously appeared on
the authors' social media accounts.

acknowledgments

thank you to mira kennedy, who so kindly took the time & energy to edit this collection. it wouldn't have been the same without your input.

thank you to summer webb & christine day, who read this collection before anyone else, & even put up with all of our questions! <3

thank you to lauren zaknoun, our wonderful cover artist, for working under time constraints & still coming up with something amazing.

finally, thank you to our guest poets, yena sharma purmasir & caitlyn siehl, for giving us the opportunity to share the work of some other awesome dragonhearted people we admire!

author bios

nikita gill is the Pushcart nominated and bestselling author of *Fierce Fairytales* and *Wild Embers*. the neighborhood children mistook her for a witch so often she decided to become one.

twitter: @nktgill
instagram: @nikita_gill

amanda lovelace is the bestselling & award-winning author of *the princess saves herself in this one* & *the witch doesn't burn in this one*. you can find her casting spells from her home in a (very) small town in central new jersey.

twitter: @ladybookmad
instagram: @ladybookmad

trista mateer is a bestselling author who occasionally crawls out of the woods to deliver manuscripts. she won the Goodreads Choice for best poetry in 2015 with her book *The Dogs I Have Kissed*.

twitter: @tristamateer
instagram: @tristamateer

more work by yena sharma purmasir can be found @yenasharmapurmasir on instagram or in her book, *When I'm Not There*, & more work by caitlyn siehl can be found @caitlynsiehl on instagram or in her book, *What We Buried*.

also by
nikita

Your Soul is a River
Wild Embers
Your Heart is the Sea
Fierce Fairytales

[Dis]connected: Poems & Stories of Connection
and Otherwise

also by
amanda

the princess saves herself in this one
the witch doesn't burn in this one

to make monsters out of girls

[Dis]connected: Poems & Stories of Connection
and Otherwise

also by
trista

Honeybee
The Dogs I Have Kissed
Before the First Kiss
Redacted

[Dis]connected: Poems & Stories of Connection
and Otherwise

Printed in Great Britain
by Amazon